EVERYTHING MEN HAVE LEARNED ABOUT WOMEN

F.J. Portera Jr.

authorHOUSE®

AuthorHouse™
1663 Liberty Drive, Suite 200
Bloomington, IN 47403
www.authorhouse.com
Phone: 1-800-839-8640

First published by AuthorHouse 11/26/2008

ISBN: 978-1-4389-2347-5 (sc)
ISBN: 978-1-4389-2348-2 (hc)

Library of Congress Control Number: 2008910863

Printed in the United States of America
Bloomington, Indiana

This book is printed on acid-free paper.

Visit:
www.mensgotoguide.com

This book is dedicated to all my friends especially Troy, Joe, Cousin Dave and my son Dominic.

I would like to thank my wife Julie for putting up with a lunatic and my daughters Natalie and Noell.

PREFACE

Finally, a book that tells it like it is. The cold, hard facts that reveal everything men have learned about women are resting between the blank pages of this book. I've taken everything you can learn from all the prominent relationship books ever written and combined and condensed them into one easy-to-understand manual every man can appreciate. This reference guide to a blissful life with women will be your new go-to guide whenever you feel the frustrations of not being able to understand how a woman thinks. In times of aggravation, simply open the book to any page and you will soon realize not only that you have never really learned anything about women in the past, but you won't learn anything today nor will you learn anything in the future.

This book isn't about the differences between men and women; this book is the quintessential summary of what men have learned by reading books that explain the differences between men and women. Combine that with the life lessons men have painfully learned over the years on their own, and what you get is a book that exemplifies the statement, "If less is more, nothing is priceless!"

This is my gift to men around the world looking to develop their knowledge of women. If you are looking for brownie points with a woman, this book is for you, and you need to keep it in plain sight so she can appreciate you trying to understand her. Having this book in your possession shows that not only do you care enough to buy a book to help you understand women, you now know that day will never come because in this profound book of what men have learned about women, you will find that nothing says "I have no idea" better than a book with nothing in it.

F.J. Portera Jr.

F.J. Portera Jr.

F.J. Portera Jr.

F.J. Portera Jr.

F.J. Portera Jr.

F.J. Portera Jr.

F.J. Portera Jr.

F.J. Portera Jr.

F.J. Portera Jr.

F.J. Portera Jr.

F.J. Portera Jr.

F.J. Portera Jr.

F.J. Portera Jr.

F.J. Portera Jr.

F.J. Portera Jr.

F.J. Portera Jr.

F.J. Portera Jr.

F.J. Portera Jr.

F.J. Portera Jr.

F.J. Portera Jr.

F.J. Portera Jr.

.

F.J. Portera Jr.

F.J. Portera Jr.

F.J. Portera Jr.

F.J. Portera Jr.

F.J. Portera Jr.

F.J. Portera Jr.

F.J. Portera Jr.

F.J. Portera Jr.

F.J. Portera Jr.

Everything Men Have Learned About Women

121

F.J. Portera Jr.

F.J. Portera Jr.

Summary

So there you have it, since the beginning of time, without even trying, women will continue to remain a mystery to men. The understanding of women has been a quest of great men throughout the perils of history, yet to this day we continue to seek on our own and incessantly come to the same conclusion… Men have learned nothing about women. Even if you think you have learned just a little something, it's usually just enough to get you into trouble… therefore you still have learned nothing. That being said, maybe it's the way it's supposed to be… maybe men were never destined to understand how a woman thinks, maybe the reason men continually fail to learn anything about women at all is the same reason that continues to keep us interested…